ALLIS-CHALMERS
MANUFACTURING CO.
10 AC 18
TRACTOR
MILWAUKEE, WISC. USA

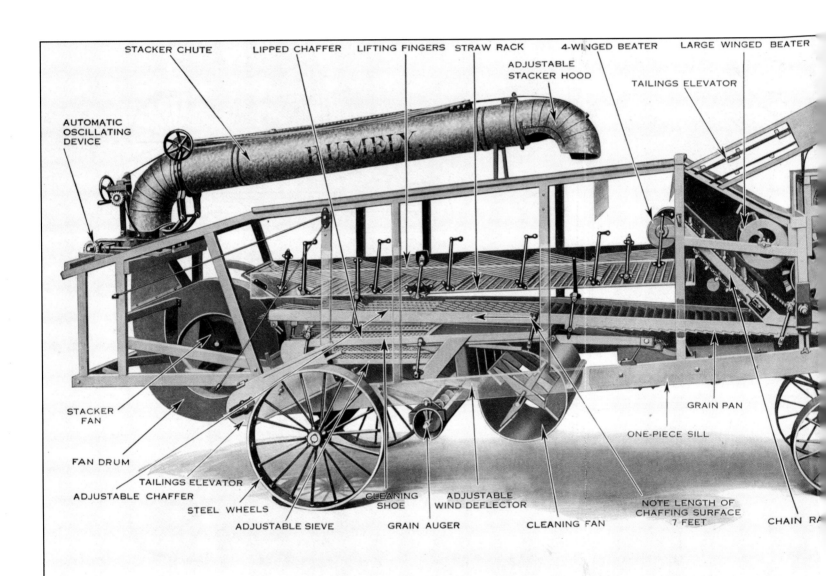

STACKER CHUTE · LIPPED CHAFFER · LIFTING FINGERS · STRAW RACK · 4-WINGED BEATER · LARGE WINGED BEATER

ADJUSTABLE STACKER HOOD

TAILINGS ELEVATOR

AUTOMATIC OSCILLATING DEVICE

STACKER FAN

FAN DRUM

TAILINGS ELEVATOR

ADJUSTABLE CHAFFER

STEEL WHEELS

ADJUSTABLE SIEVE

CLEANING SHOE

ADJUSTABLE WIND DEFLECTOR

GRAIN AUGER

CLEANING FAN

GRAIN PAN

ONE-PIECE SILL

NOTE LENGTH OF CHAFFING SURFACE 7 FEET

CHAIN RA...

SKELETON VIEW OF RUMELY IDEAL SEPARATOR

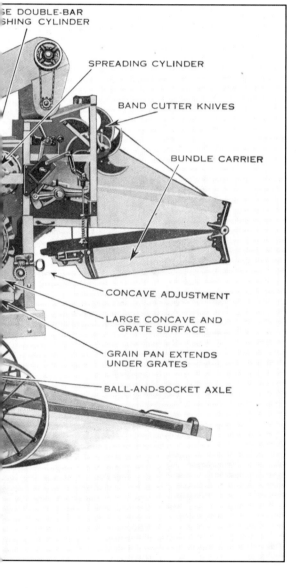

GE DOUBLE-BAR
SHING CYLINDER

SPREADING CYLINDER

BAND CUTTER KNIVES

BUNDLE CARRIER

CONCAVE ADJUSTMENT

LARGE CONCAVE AND
GRATE SURFACE

GRAIN PAN EXTENDS
UNDER GRATES

BALL-AND-SOCKET AXLE

Motorbooks International

FARM TRACTOR COLOR HISTORY

ALLIS-CHALMERS TRACTORS

Text by C. H. Wendel
Photography by Andrew Morland

Acknowledgments

Thanks to all the Allis-Chalmers tractor owners and enthusiasts whose help and cooperation made this book possible. Special thanks to the following for allowing me to photograph their tractors:

Albin Murawski, Royce Schulz, Ivan Henderson, Theodore Buisker, Marvin Holmes, John Becker, Alan Cannings, G. Stephens, Edwin and Larry Karg, William Deppe, Jim Polacek, Alan Draper, and Norm Meinert.

Also thanks to the organizers of the Old Time Threshing & Antique Engine Show at Freeport, Illinois, the Great Dorset Steam Fair, Blandford, Great Britain, and the Great Canadian Antique Farm Field Days at the Ontario Agricultural Museum.

Special thanks to Nan Jones of *Old Allis News* for help with the research. *Old Allis News* is published quarterly, available from—Pleasant Knoll, 10925 Love Road, Bellevue, Michigan 49021.

First published in 1992 by Motorbooks International Publishers & Wholesalers, PO Box 2, 729 Prospect Avenue, Osceola, WI 54020 USA

© C.H. Wendel, text, and Andrew Morland, photographs, 1992

Motorbooks International books are also available at discounts in bulk quantity for industrial or sales-promotional use. For details write to Special Sales Manager at the Publisher's address

Library of Congress Cataloging-in-Publication Data
Wendel, C. H. (Charles H.)
    Allis-Chalmers tractors / C.H. Wendel, Andrew Morland.
        p.   cm.—(Motorbooks International farm tractor color history)
    Includes index.
    ISBN 0-87938-628-2
    1. Allis-Chalmers tractors—
History.   2. Allis-Chalmers
    Corporation—History.   I. Morland,
Andrew.   II. Title.
III. Series.
TL233.5.W447   1992
629.225—dc20   92-1755

Printed in Hong Kong

On the front cover: A 1954 Allis-Chalmers WD-45 with hydraulic power and power-adjustable rear wheels.

On the back cover: A 1914 Allis-Chalmers 10-18 tractor and a Rumely OilPull.

On the frontispiece: The spectacularly restored red gas tank and green kerosene tank of Norm Meinert's 1914 Allis-Chalmers 10-18.

On the title pages: Skeleton view of the workings of the Rumely Ideal separator.

Contents

Introduction

This book presented me with several difficult problems. Although I always have felt a genuine need for a book delineating Allis-Chalmers products in glorious color, I previously compiled *The Allis-Chalmers Story* (1988: Crestline Publishing Company). That book delves into many aspects of Allis-Chalmers and covers the tractor line with more detail than is possible here. But it has black-and-white illustrations. Even though the illustrations number into the thousands, they are still black-and-white. On the other hand, this book is compiled primarily of color illustrations. The problem for me has been to define a balance between the two books.

Hopefully, readers will see this book as a companion volume. *The Allis-*

The front radiator, hood, and exhaust pipes of the Model K crawler speak of the power and strength that the A-C line was famous for.

Chalmers Story presents a detailed history of A-C products and their development; this book presents a capsulized history, but has the benefit of full-color illustrations wherever possible. The color illustrations, I hope, will also be helpful to interested collectors and restorers of vintage tractors.

The history of Allis-Chalmers includes a great many corporate tragedies. Going back to Edward P. Allis' first pumping engines of the 1870s, we see tremendous problems that ultimately resulted in large financial losses, but which were finally overcome with great success.

The 1901 merger that brought four large companies together as Allis-Chalmers also created many problems, especially since the four combined firms had far more manufacturing capacity than was necessary. The new firm had to make the tough decision of closing factories and cutting out the lines that were unprofitable or unnecessary. Eventually, Allis-Chalmers went into receivership.

When General Otto H. Falk took over in 1913, he was faced with the task of putting the company back onto a sound footing.

Under the leadership of General Falk, Allis-Chalmers came into a time of tranquility that lasted into the 1960s. Also under his leadership, Allis-Chalmers entered the farm tractor and equipment industry, going up against companies that had been building farm equipment for decades. Yet changes were taking place in the industry and on the farm.

Perhaps some of the designs were not well received by the farmer, and perhaps the company should have been more cognizant of changes in the industry. Perhaps management should have allocated more money to research and development of new equipment. "Perhaps" and "maybe" are words that often are used in hindsight. For Allis-Chalmers, the questions will forever abound as to what might have been.

Chapter 1

The History of Allis-Chalmers

Edward P. Allis and a Century-Long Chronicle of Mergers

Of all the companies destined for prominence in the farm equipment industry, Allis-Chalmers was an unlikely prospect. Until about 1912 it does not appear that diversifying into the farm tractor business ever came up. Only after General Falk was appointed as receiver of Allis-Chalmers in 1913 did the company make any overt moves in this direction.

Allis-Chalmers was incorporated in 1901. This company resulted from the merger of several large companies. The "Allis" portion came from Edward P. Allis

Looking forward from the drawbar, little is visible on this 1914 Allis-Chalmers 10-18 except for tanks and fenders. Allis-Chalmers built the two-cylinder opposed engine that offered a 5¹⁄₄x7in bore and stroke. In all, it weighed 4,800lb. Although the company lists this tractor from 1914 to 1923, it appears that most of the production occurred in the first four or five years, with the remaining years being used to sell off the existing warehouse stock. This 10-18 was restored and is owned by Norm Meinert of Davis, Illinois. This tractor carries serial number 2078.

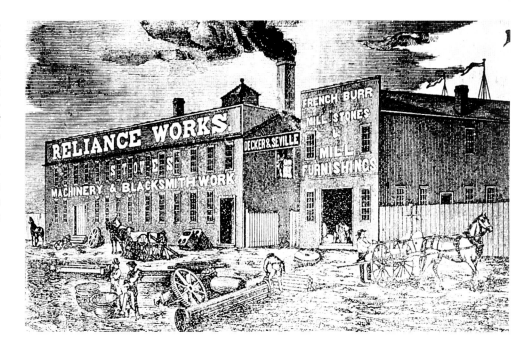

The Reliance Works of Edward P. Allis was an outgrowth of the original Decker & Seville factory. Eventually, the company became a major supplier of flour mills, sawmills, and stationary steam engines. Each of these three divisions was under the control of an eminent expert. Despite the company's many successful ventures, Allis went bankrupt in 1873, largely due to a financial panic of the time. After reorganizing, the company once again regained solvency and continued building its quality products, almost without interruption.

Edward P. Allis came to Milwaukee in 1846. Eleven years later he purchased the bankrupt firm of Decker & Seville and put himself into the foundry business. In addition, the company built stone buhr mills and dressed millstones. Under Allis' leadership, the company continued to grow. During the 1880s, Allis was fortunate enough to obtain the services of eminent experts in the company's various endeavors, which put the company into a position of prominence. Subsequently, hard times and changing markets helped to bring about the formation of the Allis-Chalmers Company in 1901.

who formed his own company in 1861. He bought out the firm of Decker & Seville in Milwaukee, Wisconsin, which had begun in 1847. In 1869, Allis bought out the Bay State Iron Manufacturing Company.

The Edward P. Allis Company made iron castings. When Allis successfully bid on supplying 2,600 tons of pipe for the Milwaukee water system, he achieved prominence in his field. Allis was also the successful bidder in supplying steam-operated pumps for the new system.

The "Chalmers" portion of the company name came from the 1901 merger in which the firm of Fraser & Chalmers was a player. This firm had been organized in 1872, and had roots reaching back to 1842. Fraser & Chalmers gained fame with its rock-crushing equipment.

Another party to the consolidation was the Gates Iron Works, also builders of rock crushers and equipment. This company was established in 1872 and, like Fraser & Chalmers, traced its roots back to the Gates Iron Works founded in 1842.

William Dixon Gray headed the Flour Milling Department of the Edward P. Allis Company. Gray joined Allis in 1877. At this time, virtually all flour was ground between buhrstones. Thus, the company was continuously busy with men shaping new ones. In 1877, the company began importing a roller-type flour mill. From this began a series of developments that revolutionized the milling industry. A substantial number of Allis mills remain in operation today.

The other major contributor to the Allis-Chalmers merger of 1901 was the Dickson Manufacturing Company. This firm had been organized in 1846, and built an extensive series of steam boilers, tanks, and other equipment.

Beginning as a custom foundry, the Edward P. Allis Company later specialized in making cast-iron pipe, and then decided to build the pumps to supply the new water mains they were manufacturing. The initial Hamilton-Corliss engines came in over budget, and Allis was not satisfied with Hamilton's engineering methods, although Hamilton was considered to be an eminent engineer.

In 1877, Allis hired Edwin Reynolds to take over the steam department. Under his leadership, the Reynolds-Corliss engines became among the finest ever built. In fact, Reynolds went so far as to retrofit existing steam engines with the Reynolds-Corliss system; an idea that helped the company gain a foothold in an already competitive market.

Within a few years, the Edward P. Allis Company offered an enormous selection of Reynolds-Corliss engines—everything from relatively small models of the 100hp class, ranging up to gigantic engines of several thousand horsepower. The company's Manhattan engines, built for the New York rapid transit subway system, were among the largest ever built.

In the Manhattan engines, four cylinders were used. The two high-pressure cylinders carried a 44in bore. After being partially expanded in the high-pressure cylinders, the steam was exhausted to huge low-pressure cylinders having a diameter of 88in. All cylinders had a common stroke of 60in. Nine of these huge engines were installed for the rapid transit system. They drove the huge generators which in turn powered the entire subway. When all nine engines were on line, the boilers required 1,000 tons of coal every twenty-four hours.

The company's Steam Division eventually entered the steam turbine field, and the Internal Combustion Engine Division built not only some of the largest gas engines, but also built nu-

The company's Sawmill Division received its impetus from George M. Hinkley, who worked for Allis from 1873 until his death in 1905. At the time of his death, Hinkley had garnered over thirty-five patents relating to sawmill machinery. Perfection of the band mill was his crowning achievement and remains a monument to his inventive genius.

Edwin Reynolds began his career with the famous Corliss Steam Engine Company of Providence, Rhode Island. He also installed the gigantic Corliss engine featured in Machinery Hall at the 1876 American Centennial Exposition. A year later, Allis hired Reynolds. Shortly afterward, the first Reynolds-Corliss steam engine appeared. Subsequently, the Reynolds-Corliss became synonymous with the ultimate in engine designs.

Designed by Edwin Reynolds, the huge Manhattan engines were, at the time, the largest steam engines ever built. These huge engines drove electric generators, and they in turn powered the enormous New York subway system. In addition to the Manhattan engines, Allis also built large pumping engines of virtually every description. By 1905, Allis-Chalmers was making headway with relatively new steam turbines, and this spelled the beginning of the end for the Reynolds-Corliss engine.

merous and innovative stationary diesel engines.

Another important part of the company was the Sawmill Division. It came into its own when George M. Hinkley went to work for Allis in 1873. Under Hinkley's direction, Allis built huge band sawmills and all types of related sawmill machinery. Large logging operations extensively used these huge sawmills. By the 1920s, sales had dropped to a fraction of earlier days. The Allis mills were so well built that they didn't wear out.

William Gray formed another company division in 1877. Under his direction, flour milling was revolutionized with the inception of the roller mill. Prior to this time, flour was milled between stone buhrs and the best flour came from French buhrstones. These imported

stone blocks were carefully shaped and dressed. However, even the best buhrstone mills left the bran in the flour; Allis' roller mill prevented this problem.

Within a few years, the Edward P. Allis Company supplied roller mills and flour mill machinery to companies all over the world. As with the Sawmill Division, the Flour Mill Division came into hard times by the 1920s. The company had reached the saturation point for new installations, and existing ones required only normal maintenance and repair. Thus, this important division was essentially reduced to a parts supply house.

After the 1901 merger formed Allis-Chalmers, the company billed itself as the "Company of the Four Powers—Steam, Gas, Water, and Electricity."

Just as Allis-Chalmers had built some of the largest steam engines in the world, so also did the company build some of the world's largest internal combustion engines. Beginning with experimental work in 1902, Allis-Chalmers soon developed a 1,000hp engine. Within a few years the company was capable of building engines ranging up to 10,000hp. One such engine was delivered to the Illinois Steel Company in 1929. Each cylinder weighed 168,000lb; each connecting rod weighed 30,500lb! The 26ft flywheel weighed 185,000lb; its rated speed was 83½rpm. From a standstill, it took less than two minutes to bring one of these engines up to its rated speed.

After the 1901 merger, Allis-Chalmers moved quickly to diversify its operations. Their scope was already wide, since by the time of the merger, flour mills, Corliss engines, rock crushers, pumping machinery, boilers, and saw-mills were among the major divisions.

Allis-Chalmers saw great opportunities in the infantile electrical power business. Huge electrical generators had already been coupled directly to Reynolds-Corliss steam engines, and now it seemed appropriate to manufacture this equipment rather than buy it from another builder.

Thus, in 1904 the Bullock Electrical & Manufacturing Company was taken over; it had originated as the Card Electric Motor & Dynamo Company in 1887. The only other major acquisition of this period was buying out the air brake business of Christensen Engineering Company in 1906. However, competition in this endeavor was fierce, and the company did little with railway air brakes.

By 1912 the company was in serious financial straits, and soon went into receivership. From its ashes came the Allis-Chalmers Manufacturing Company. Under the able leadership of General Otto Falk, the new corporation was soon back on its feet. Falk phased out some portions of the company and combined others. By 1923 the entire production of Allis-Chalmers was coming from two plants, where previously there had been six.

As previously pointed out, the major divisions that had been responsible for the company's growth would also be the cause for difficult times in the 1920s and later. Thus, it was a stroke of genius on the part of General Falk when he directed the company toward the farm machinery business. Prior to Falk's 1932 retirement, the company had purchased five different companies involved in the farm machinery business, plus numerous others whose products were beneficial to the overall operation of the corporation.

In 1928, Allis-Chalmers took over the Monarch Tractor Corporation, ostensibly to bolster its new line of construction machinery. However, some of the A-C Monarch tractors were also sold for

Texrope Drives were first announced in March 1925. Originally intended to obviate the problems with textile mill drives, the Texrope system was developed by Walter Geist, who would later become president of Allis-Chalmers. Although the v-belt drive had been used prior to this time, the Texrope Drive was the beginning of the multiple v-belt drive system. Between the development of the electric motor and the development of the Texrope drive, flat pulleys, leather belts, and line shafts soon found their way to the scrap pile and the history books.

farm use. LaCrosse Plow Company was added to the list in 1929, and Stearns Engine Company followed a year later. In 1931, Allis-Chalmers bought out the Advance-Rumely Thresher Company and the Birdsell Manufacturing Company.

Numerous acquisitions followed, with the 1953 buy out of Buda Corporation of Harvey, Illinois, giving the company a major boost because it provided them with their own engine plant. Another important purchase was that of the

Gleaner Corporation in 1955. This put Allis-Chalmers in the forefront of the major American combine builders.

Despite many innovations, and despite numerous model changes during the years, Allis-Chalmers succumbed to many of the same problems that have besieged farm equipment companies over the years. In 1974 Allis-Chalmers and Fiat of Italy merged forces in the crawler tractor and construction machinery business. This resulted in the firm of

This Allis-Chalmers 10-18 tractor was built at the West Allis, Wisconsin, works in 1914. The 10-18 was equipped with a single gear forward and a single reverse. Allis-Chalmers announced this tractor in November 1914, in anticipation of the 1915 crop season. A major talking point called it "the only tractor that has a one-piece steel heat-treated frame—no rivets to work loose—will not sag under the heaviest strains." The 10-18's three-wheel design was popular at the time, and several other companies were building tractors with a vaguely similar appearance.

15

Fiat-Allis. Since Allis-Chalmers was a minority shareholder in the new corporation, the A-C presence in this industry dimmed by 1975.

Likewise, the farm equipment lines suffered one setback after another. Slowly but gradually, various aspects of the line disappeared. The calamitous decline of the agricultural economy in the early 1980s completely upset the farm equipment industry, and Allis-Chalmers fell victim to the times. On March 29, 1985, Allis-Chalmers sold its farm equipment line to Klockner-Humboldt-Deutz AG of Germany.

Another view of the Allis-Chalmers 10-18 shows off the unique three-wheel design. Also visible is the engine flywheel, clutch, and transmission case. Since the engine was cross-mounted on the frame, it was easy to carry the power through the clutch and directly into the transmission case. Then, a series of spur gears transmitted power to the drive wheels. The red tank at the top is for gasoline to be used when starting the engine. Below it is a much larger tank to carry kerosene. After the engine was warmed up on gasoline, it was switched over for burning kerosene fuel. Most companies used this method of operation up to about 1940.

Allis-Chalmers put forth a lot of effort toward making the little 6-12 tractor a success. This factory scene illustrates a Russell Junior grader attached to the 6-12. The Russell Grader Manufacturing Company of Minneapolis, Minnesota, built the grader. Despite A-C's herculean efforts, farmer acceptance of the 6-12 was poor. When Allis-Chalmers saw the light and began building a conventional unit-frame tractor design, the company was on its way to success in the industry.

Built in the 1918-1926 period, the Allis-Chalmers 6-12 used what might be called a semi-articulated design. When equipped with the sulky as shown here, it used a center hinge for steering. When coupled to another machine such as a grain binder, the binder's wheels functioned in the same manner as the sulky attachment. The Moline Universal was another tractor of this general design, and it, like the 6-12 shown here, met with mild popularity for a few years. Carrying serial number 10655, this tractor was built about 1919. Unfortunately, company records for this model no longer exist.

Shown here is Norm Meinert of Davis, Illinois, at the controls of his rare 6-12 Allis-Chalmers tractor. Meinert specializes in collecting and restoring Allis-Chalmers tractors. This side view illustrates the sulky attachment for the 6-12. If a farmer wanted the tractor to pull a grain binder, then the binder would take the place of the sulky. The problem was that most farmers weren't interested in the work required to change over from one implement to another. They preferred to line up the holes, drop in a drawbar pin, and be on their way.

Close examination shows what happens during a turn with the 6-12 tractor. The "torque tube" is connected to a pivot device directly to the back of the tractor engine. All other tractor controls were operated from the seat, and in the case of other equipment, extensions to the control rods permitted one-man operation in many instances. This design was protected under patent number 1,419,113 issued in 1922. It was the brainchild of J.M.F. Patitz, the eminent steam turbine engineer at Allis-Chalmers.

This close-up view illustrates the seat and driving controls for the 6-12 tractors. Once aboard the seat, the steering wheel, clutch, gear shift, and throttle were all in easy reach of the operator. Plows, harrows, cultivators, and potato-diggers were some of the implements attached beneath the torque tube. This placed the operator in the best possible field of vision. Another attachment was the modification of a mower so that the operator sat in his usual position, but instead of horses being the power source, the little 6-12 tractor pulled the mower.

The powerplant in the 6-12 tractor was a little LeRoi Model 20 four-cylinder engine. It was built in Milwaukee, not far from the A-C factories. The 3⅛x4½in bore and stroke yielded about 6 drawbar and 12 brake horsepower, thus the 6-12 rating. Note the air cleaner in use on this engine. By 1920, some tractors were using an air cleaner of one style or another, but many continued to run with an open air pipe, or at best, raised the air intake a few feet in order to keep the larger chunks of dirt, chaff, and bugs out of the engine.

This close-up view illustrates the placement of the belt pulley. Directly above is the quadrant and pinion working around the articulated joint. The steering wheel terminated in the small pinion, and as it turned the steering position changed relative to the quadrant. When lining up to a belt, it was a clever trick to get the tractor in the proper lateral position and then "steer" the tractor so as to tighten it. Even then, it beat dragging a heavy stationary engine into position and driving enough stakes into the ground to keep it there.

Inside the Allis-Chalmers factory in 1918 with the first of the new 15-30 tractors in production. The sleek new design of the 15-30 was a major departure from the unconventional design of the 10-18 and 6-12 models. A few months after its introduction, the 15-30 was rated upward to 18-30, meaning that this tractor could deliver 18 drawbar and 30 belt horsepower. Standard colors for the 18-30 included a deep green body.

Inside the Allis-Chalmers factory more than fifty years later with the D-19 tractors in the final stages of assembly. Although the exact date of this photograph is unknown, it was taken between 1961 and 1963, the only years A-C built the D-19. Industry critics sometimes called the A-C tractor production facilities outdated, yet until production ended in 1985, Allis-Chalmers maintained an excellent record of quality control and competitive pricing.

OILPULL

Highest
Powered-
Lightest
Weight

Chapter 2

Advance Rumely Tractors 1857-1931

From the OilPull to the DoAll, a Long Lineage of Innovation

When Allis-Chalmers bought out the Advance-Rumely Thresher Company in 1931, A-C was squarely into the farm equipment business. Prior to this time, A-C limped along as a farm tractor builder, but lacking the necessary dealer organization and branch houses, it was virtually impossible to gain a real foothold in what had become a competitive business.

Meinrad Rumely was a German immigrant who settled in La Porte, Indiana, in 1852. His blacksmith shop and foundry soon began building small grain threshers. Their quality was undisputed,

Although the majority of the OilPull tractors were finished in a dark green enamel, the last years of production saw the OilPull in a steel gray enamel, but still with red wheels. The exact reason for the change has never been answered. Some suggest that Advance-Rumely came up with a large amount of gray paint at a bargain price, and thus the change. Like many other farm equipment companies of the 1920s and early 1930s, Advance-Rumely was in desperate financial straits, finally selling out to Allis-Chalmers in 1931.

This 8hp Rumely portable steam engine is of 1880s vintage, and perhaps even earlier. Meinrad Rumely began building small wooden threshers in La Porte, Indiana, in 1852. Since this engine carries the legend "M. & J. Rumely" in the heater casting, it was built between 1872 and 1882. The firm operated under this title until 1882. The earlier date marks the building of Rumely's first portable steam engine, although Rumely had begun building threshing machines some thirty years before.

This 1917 photograph illustrates the Advance-Rumely Universal steam engine in the 25hp size. This one is equipped with a canopy and a side tank for additional water. Rumely topped its steam engine line with a gigantic 40hp size built between 1905 and 1908. During this time, engine builders acquired the contagion of trying to build the largest steam engine. Since they were suitable only for the very largest work on the open prairies, the sale of these engines was limited.

and within a few years Meinrad and his brother John were getting more orders than they could handle.

The business grew rapidly. In 1882, Meinrad bought out his brother's interest, and the new company was known as

M. Rumely Company. Edward Rumely, Meinrad's grandson, took the reins of the company in 1907. Following his vision, Rumely soon entered the tractor business with the OilPull tractor on February 21, 1910.

The success of the OilPull engine was in its unique design. The engine's compression ratio was somewhat higher than in contemporary tractors. The oil coolant permitted a higher jacket temperature than was possible with a water coolant. The unique design of the cooling system permitted virtually automatic temperature regulation depending on the engine load. Due to this unique design feature, the OilPull engine was able to successfully burn kerosene at any load and under any conditions. This claim

could not be made successfully by any other builder.

Several major acquisitions and significant crop failures led to financial embarrassment, and the company became insolvent in 1915. It was reorganized as Advance-Rumely Thresher Company, and remained in business until 1931. During this sixteen-year period, Advance-Rumely built essentially the same equipment as before.

The OilPull tractors saw various modifications, including the 1924 changeover to the so-called Lightweight design. Essentially though, the design was still the same. Perhaps from lack of research money, or perhaps from an unwillingness to toss out a proven design, Advance-Rumely stood still while

A Rumely company photo illustrates a preproduction model of the famous OilPull tractor, nicknamed Kerosene Annie. Development of this tractor began in 1908, and perhaps even earlier. Several prototypes were built between 1908 and 1910, and Rumely employees went to work in a brand new OilPull tractor factory on February 21, 1910. The initial offering was the Type B, rated at 25 drawbar and 45 belt horsepower. The two cylinders carried a 9½in bore and a 12in stroke.

RUMELY 15-30 OILPULL TRACTOR
The Guaranteed Kerosene Burner

Advance-Rumely

After successful launching of the Type B OilPull, Rumely began offering additional styles. Included was this 15-30 Type F tractor. It carried a list price of about $3,000, a substantial figure for a farmer to pay at the time. Despite the price, the OilPull line gained an excellent reputation right from the start. Before long, the OilPull name carried with it a certain inexplicable mystique that persists to this day. Even though OilPull tractors have been out of production for sixty years, they still remain among the most popular with vintage tractor enthusiasts.

29

many competitors developed unit-frame tractors, and moved on to row-crop designs.

By the 1930s, Advance-Rumely was in danger of losing everything without the possibility of a merger. When Allis-Chalmers took over in 1931, the Advance-Rumely corporate identity ended. From the ashes, A-C built its own chapter in the farm equipment industry.

The Rumely OilPull tractors all used the large square radiator that came to typify the design. Inside the radiator were a large number of thin sections that permitted maximum radiation of heat to the surrounding air. The engine exhaust created an induced draft. The exhaust pipes terminated in vertical nozzles placed inside the stack. The harder the engine worked, the heavier the draft. Thus, maintaining the cylinder temperature was virtually automatic, without the use of fans, thermostats, and other devices. This OilPull is owned by the Ontario, Canada, Agricultural Museum at Milton.

RUMELY
OilPull
TRACTOR
LA PORTE, IND.
REG.U.S.PAT.OFF.

GUARANTEED
TO BURN SUCCESSFULLY ALL GRADES OF KERO-
SENE UNDER ALL CONDITIONS, AT ALL LOADS
UP TO ITS RATED BRAKE HORSE POWER.

The Rumely OilPull tractors were distinguished among other things, by the square, boxlike radiator. The guarantee reads, "Guaranteed to burn successfully all grades of kerosene under any conditions, at all loads up to its rated brake horsepower." Part of the OilPull success was in the use of an oil coolant; this permitted the higher cylinder jacket temperatures necessary to successfully burn kerosene and other low-grade fuels. Within the history of the farm equipment industry, few trademarks are recognized more quickly than that of the famous OilPull. Already in 1909, the M. Rumely Company had developed prototypes of the design. Under the able leadership of John Secor and William Higgins, the OilPull design came to life. Of course, all this was under the direction of Edward A. Rumely.

8227

The OilPull tractor saw numerous changes during its long production run. However, the farmer of the 1920s longed for a row-crop tractor, and the OilPull design was not being modified in that direction. Advance-Rumely did, however, make major changes to the OilPull in 1924; this was the Type S 30-60, built 1924-1928. A pressed-steel frame replaced the structural steel framework of earlier years. This change gave great strength with a fraction of the weight found before. Later models included many unique and interesting features, including a rear wheel differential lock.

Next page
Built only in 1930 and 1931, the Rumely 6A tractor saw very limited numbers; when Allis-Chalmers took over in 1931, over 700 tractors were still in the warehouse. A-C continued advertising these tractors until remaining stocks were depleted, thus this model was listed in various tractor directories as late as 1934. This copy was built in 1930. Owner Royce Schulz of Monroe, Wisconsin, beautifully restored this model.

Since production was limited on this Rumely model, few have survived, and existing examples are scarce. The smooth-running, six-cylinder engine provided nearly 50hp on the belt, making this an ideal tractor for use with a threshing machine. Here's Marc Blanc driving his grandfather's Rumely 6 at the Old Time Threshing & Antique Engine Show, Freeport, Illinois. Marc is the grandson of Royce Schulz of Monroe, Wisconsin.

A front view of the Rumely 6 shows the arched front axle. The arched axle permitted the tractor to straddle a row without damaging young crops. Rumely 6 tractors were equipped with a Waukesha engine built to the specifications of Advance-Rumely. Thus, many parts are not interchangeable with concurrent Waukesha engines. Rated at 1365rpm, this engine used a $4^{1}/_{4}$x$4^{3}/_{4}$in bore and stroke. Total weight was 6,370lb.

A close look at this Rumely 6 illustrates front and rear lighting equipment. This was original road equipment optionally available with these tractors. A belt-driven generator provided the electricity. It should be noted, however, that the Ford Model T front wheels are definitely not factory equipment. This Rumely 6 is owned by Albin Murawski of Port Austin, Michigan.

Next page
Although the Waukesha Motor Company built the Rumely 6 engine, the exhaust manifold nevertheless carried Advance-Rumely cast into place. A large 6 is also cast into the manifold as an overt reference to its six-cylinder design. It should be remembered that the majority of tractors built in 1930 carried two- or four-cylinder engines; and very few carried a six-cylinder motor. In 1930, Advance-Rumely built tractors serial number 501 and 502. The following year, tractors 503 to 1302 were built. By the time Allis-Chalmers took over in late 1931, Advance-Rumely had sold less than a hundred copies, with the other 700 plus tractors remaining in the warehouse.

Previous page
Rumely 6 tractors used a distinctive trademark, in this case, on the top radiator tank. Advance-Rumely continued marketing their OilPull tractors right up to the 1931 Allis-Chalmers buy out. The Rumely 6 design came along late in Rumely history, perhaps too late to have been a serious contender for industry dominance. Like most farm machinery builders, Advance-Rumely saw tough economic times during the postwar depression of the early 1920s. Although not yet broken as a result, Rumely was severely bent by these events, and this kept Rumely, like many others, from spending large sums on development of lightweight tractors.

A platform view of the Rumely 6 illustrates its simplicity of design. (Even in Rumely's own advertising, the terms Rumely 6 and Rumely Six were used interchangeably.) In Nebraska test number 185, the Rumely 6 was rated at 1365rpm, a high crank speed for its day. The majority of 1930 model tractors operated at speeds under 1200rpm. The above test revealed a maximum pull of 4,273lb at 2.95mph for a yield of 33.57 drawbar horsepower. In other words, the Rumely 6 pulled about 67 percent of its own weight.

Next page
Advance-Rumely acquired the Toro motor cultivator line about 1927. From it they built the Rumely DoAll tractor, first announced in 1928. The DoAll was yet another of the convertible tractors that were evident in the tractor market during the 1920s. Many tractor builders designed what they thought the farmer needed, rather than building what farmers wanted. The problem then became one of convincing the farmer that he needed the tractor, even though the farmer wasn't convinced he wanted it. Finally, the industry concluded that building what the farmer wanted was the secret to success.

and NOW the New RUMELY DoAll

$995.00 CASH
F.O.B. FACTORY
COMPLETE WITH TWO-ROW CULTIVATING EQUIPMENT

A Combined Cultivating and Plowing Tractor Completely Equipped

Ready for Every Field Operation from Plowing to Cultivating

Terms, if desired, at a slightly increased price

IT IS now our privilege to present the Rumely DoAll Tractor, another new product of Advance-Rumely engineering skill worthy of the best traditions of the name it bears—a combined plowing and cultivating power unit, designed to fill a long-felt need on farms of all sizes. Like all Rumely machinery, it is the result of long experience in designing and building dependable farm equipment, and present indications are that its reception will exceed that accorded any previous Rumely product.

The Rumely DoAll as a conventional four-wheel tractor. If cultivating equipment is not wanted, the DoAll can be purchased in this form at a corresponding lower price.

ONE year ago the new 20-30 Super-Powered OilPull Tractor was announced to the agricultural world. The response was immediate and overwhelming. Orders for the new product poured in from all parts of Canada and the United States and from abroad. Our factories were swamped and are still taxed to the limit of their facilities to supply the demand. It was a singular demonstration of confidence in the name RUMELY and all that it stands for.

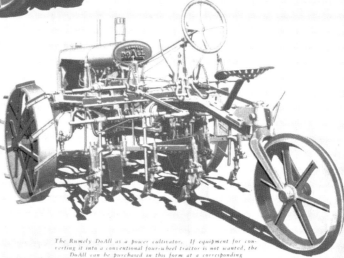

The Rumely DoAll as a power cultivator. If equipment for converting it into a conventional four-wheel tractor is not wanted, the DoAll can be purchased in this form at a corresponding reduction in price.

RUMELY IDEAL SEPARATOR
Equipped with Feeder, Weigher and Windstacker

M. Rumely Company, and its successor, Advance-Rumely Thresher Company, gained an enviable position in the industry with their Rumely Ideal separator. Its roots went back to 1852 with Meinrad Rumely's first crude thresher. Production of various Ideal threshers continued until the company was bought out by Allis-Chalmers in 1931. Rumely introduced an all-steel thresher in 1916, and the all-wood construction was gradually phased out.

For several years after the 1931 buy out of Advance-Rumely, the Allis-Chalmers dealers offered threshing machines. Apparently, this was limited to assembly of machines from the existing parts inventory, along with the sale of threshing machines from warehouse inventories. Since Allis-Chalmers was concurrently involved with the development and promotion of their radically new All-Crop combine, they had little interest in pushing the sale of new threshing machines. This illustration is significant in that it combines Allis-Chalmers and Rumely on the same piece of equipment.

THE **RUMELY**

HILLSIDE COMBINE

Three-quarter left-hand view of the Rumely No. 3 Hillside Combine.

AN IDEAL HARVESTER FOR HILLY COUNTRY

Advance-Rumely announced its first combine in 1925. Several different models appeared in the following years, but production essentially ended when Allis-Chalmers bought out Rumely in 1931. After all, the A-C approach was entirely different. They developed a small, lightweight, and affordable combine that was within the means of most farmers, and still didn't require forty acres just to turn around. Advance-Rumely combines were built in Prairie and Hillside models.

Chapter 3

Monarch Tractors 1913-1928

A Short Odyssey of the Treaded Crawler Tractors

Monarch first saw light in 1913 as a small company in Watertown, Wisconsin. During 1919, the company was reorganized as Monarch Tractors Incorporated, and appears to have been headed for the Chicago area for a short time under the title of General Tractors Incorporated. Then, in 1925 the company resurfaced in Springfield, Illinois, as Monarch Tractors.

It appears that Monarch contacted Allis-Chalmers regarding the possibility of a merger sometime in 1927. When these discussions led to a merger on February 27, 1928, Allis-Chalmers began a half-century odyssey in the crawler tractor business. This ended in 1974 with a merger forming Fiat-Allis Construction Machinery, Incorporated.

The Model WM crawler shown in these photographs is owned by Alan Draper of Bishopstone of Salisbury, Wiltshire, Great Britain. This nicely restored copy is complete with the engine side panels. In the field, however, many of the side panels were removed to provide better engine cooling. A-C built two versions of the Model M crawler. The earlier style, built until 1937, used a four-cylinder engine with a $4^3/8$x5in bore and stroke. Later models carried an engine with an increased bore of $4^1/2$in.

In 1928, A-C got into the crawler tractor business in a big way by purchasing Monarch Tractors, which had gained a wide reputation in previous years. In fact, the A-C crawler line embodied many Monarch features. Shown here is a Monarch 50 pulling a five-yard crawler dump wagon built by Austin-Western. The high flotation of the crawler, plus the added flotation afforded by the dump wagon permitted working in conditions that would have been totally impossible by wheeled tractors and equipment.

Allis-Chalmers acquired Monarch Tractors of Springfield, Illinois, in 1928. This 1934 A-C Model K crawler was originally developed as the Monarch 35. Production of this model continued until 1943. This nicely restored Model K is owned by Alan Draper of Great Britain. In this design the front portion of the tracks are attached to a huge leaf spring beneath the engine. The spring absorbed operating shocks, and permitted a limited amount of flexibility between the two tracks. The heavy grille was required equipment, since operating among trees and brush without it would be suicide for the delicate radiator core.

A typical application of the agricultural crawler was for plowing, as is shown here with Alan Draper's Model K tractor. Allis-Chalmers sold a fair number of these crawlers for agricultural purposes, and went so far as to offer a special Orchard Model. The Orchard Model used the same engine and chassis as the standard model, but the intake and exhaust pipes, as well as some of the operating controls, were moved to a low position. This Model K crawler is of 1934 vintage and still used the steering wheel control, a design used up through serial number 4451 of 1935. In this same year, Allis-Chalmers began offering the Model K-O tractor. It used the same chassis but was equipped with an oil engine after the Hesselmann pattern. It is entirely possible that this was in reality a Waukesha-Hesselmann engine, but nothing definite has emerged on this point. The K-O tractor was offered only in 1935.

The large K cast into the radiator tank's sides left indelible proof of origin for this tractor model. Allis-Chalmers tested this model at Nebraska in 1929 under number 171. The tractor used the company's own four-cylinder engine. Rated at 930rpm, it carried a $4^3/_4$x$6^1/_2$in bore and stroke. In this test it pulled 8,450lb for 40.99 maximum drawbar horsepower. Total tractor weight was 10,680lb; it pulled 79 percent of its own weight.

A close-up photo illustrates the steering system used on the Model K crawlers up to 1935. That year, the company changed the steering system to use steering levers. Various modifications were made to the Model K tractors during the production run, but most of these were cosmetic in nature. For instance, the large K cast into the radiator tank's sides on later tractors was actually a replacement for the figures 35 that had been used initially.

The Model WM crawler from Allis-Chalmers first made its appearance in 1932, with production continuing for a decade. During that time, A-C produced over 14,000 units. Not all were of the WM variety, with this designator indicating a Model M crawler with a wide track gauge. Both the standard gauge Model M and the wide-gauge WM styles are included in the basic production list. Allis-Chalmers developed this model from the earlier Monarch line, and in fact, there were features of the Monarch tractors that carried through in the A-C crawler line for many years.

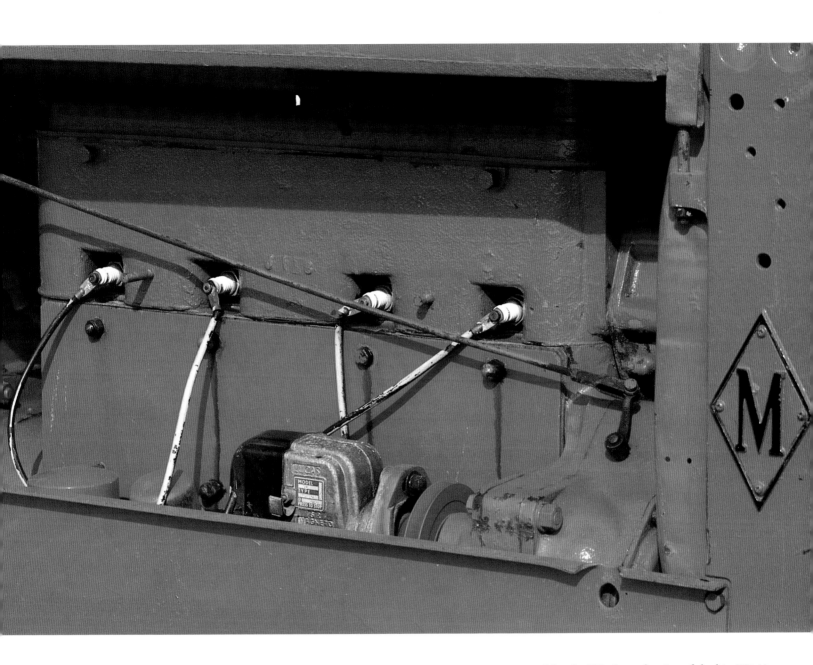

Previous page
Alan Draper's 1941 Model WM crawler is one of the few remaining examples of this crawler. Visible toward the top is the leaf spring suspension that carried the tractor's front portion. The suspension is connected to both track frames. Below is shown the huge coil spring used to tension the tracks. A tremendous amount of spring pressure is required in this situation. The tracks and rails are so heavy that coupling them, even with the springs completely backed away, requires mechanical equipment—brute strength is simply no match!

Like the HD-6, production of the big HD-11 tractor ran for the decade beginning with 1955. Standard equipment for this 122hp tractor included a six-cylinder diesel engine with a 516ci displacement. A turbocharger was standard equipment. In 1968, this tractor listed at slightly over $25,000, or just over $1 a pound.

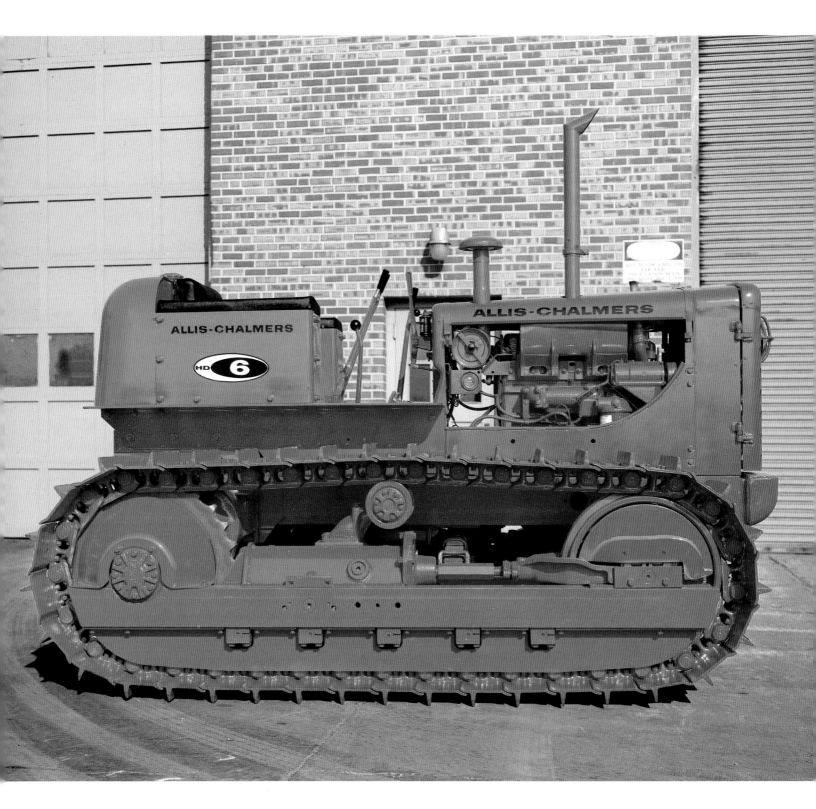

Production of the H and HD Series crawler tractors began in 1940. The line was modified and changed numerous times. A-C introduced this HD-6 tractor in 1955, with production continuing for a decade. Looking at a certain amount of agricultural use, the HD-6 was tested at Nebraska in 1956 under number 580. In 1960, this tractor carried a list price of $9,840.

A three-quarter rear view of the Model WM crawler illustrates its wide-tread design. For this model, a 50in track gauge was used, while the standard Model M crawler used a 40in track gauge. The added width dramatically increased stability when working on slopes. In addition to A-C's many attachments, numerous other companies offered aftermarket equipment, including the Hough hydraulic loader. Alan Draper is shown at the controls of his Model WM crawler. Note that one track is wider than the other. When restoring this tractor, Draper had one new 13in track, and one new 15in track, so he fitted both of these to the WM. Allis-Chalmers offered tracks ranging in width from 13 to 18in. Except for those crawlers made by Caterpillar Tractor Company, crawler tractors are not called "Caterpillars." Caterpillar, as applied to crawler tractors, is a trademark of Caterpillar Tractor Company.

Chapter 4

Allis-Chalmers Tractors 1913-1990s

The Persian Orange Tractors Lead the March of Agricultural Progress

In 1913, Allis-Chalmers was a major builder of flour mills, sawmills, and countless other machinery. In fact, the company was one of the largest industrial builders in the world. Yet it was completely unknown in the farm tractor business. When General Otto Falk took over the helm of Allis-Chalmers in 1913, he provided new directions for the com-

Allis-Chalmers UC tractors featured a four-cylinder overhead-valve engine designed by none other than Allis-Chalmers. The engine used a 4³/₈x5in bore and stroke. The Model UC was tested at Nebraska in 1935 under number 238. As with many tractors of the period, the drawbar tests were run both on steel wheels and rubber tires. For one thing, all farmers weren't yet convinced that rubber tires were the way to go, and for another, rubber tire equipment added substantially to the cost. However, a few years later most farmers wanted rubber tires because traction was better, slippage was less, and the ride was a whole lot smoother. By 1940, only a few diehards still preferred the daylong bouncing and shaking of the steel wheels from daylight until dark.

pany that included entering the farm tractor business.

Failure followed failure as the company went from the rotary tiller design of Motoculture Ltd. to the equally unimpressive tractor-truck. This wasn't the end of poor designs, either. The 10-18 never endeared itself to the American farmer, and the small 6-12 fared little better. Finally, the company developed the successful 15-30 tractor, which soon became known as the 18-30. This design was modified several times, and finally resulted in the Model E, 25-40 tractor.

Despite reasonable success with the 18-30 and other models, Allis-Chalmers sadly lacked a dealer network. This was finally resolved with the 1931 acquisition of the Advance-Rumely Thresher Company of La Porte, Indiana. A-C had no interest in Rumely's well-established Oil-Pull tractor line or in their recently developed DoAll tractor.

The major benefit of the Rumely purchase was the acquisition of a ready-made, well-established, and highly respected dealer organization. The Rumely

acquisition came with near-perfect timing, since A-C was about to release their new UC tractor, and was within months of presenting the rubber-tire tractor to the farming public.

An earlier buy out of Monarch Tractors of Springfield, Illinois, had put A-C into the crawler tractor business. While a substantial number of the new A-C Monarch crawlers found their way to farms and ranches, the majority were used for construction work. After all, Allis-Chalmers had its major background in the construction industries, and at this time, the company's greatest emphasis was placed on the heavy equipment lines, rather than on farm machinery.

In purchasing the LaCrosse Implement Company of LaCrosse, Wisconsin, A-C gained access to an already developed line of farm implements, along with a substantial number of LaCrosse dealers.

Allis-Chalmers provided many innovative firsts to the farm equipment industry:

A 4-Plow Tractor within reach of Every Farmer

- A-C used the first square engine, 4in bore and stroke in their WC tractor.
- Rubber tires were first used and sold on Allis-Chalmers tractors in 1931.
- Power-adjustable rear wheels were first used on the 1948 WD tractor.
- The D-19 Diesel was the first agricultural tractor to be equipped with a turbocharger.
- Allis-Chalmers was one of the first farm tractor companies to use a dry-type air cleaner.
- Power steering was introduced on the WD-45 tractor in 1956.
- Positive seal track idlers were announced for A-C crawler tractors in 1939.

Development work on a smaller partner for the 18-30 tractor began in 1920, with the company announcing this small 12-20 model in January 1921. Designed after the larger 18-30, it quickly revealed an output substantially higher than the initial rating, so within months the 12-20 became known as the 15-25. Production of this tractor continued until 1927. It was also available as an orchard tractor with special fenders and related orchard equipment. About 1921, the 18-30 tractor was modified and re-rated as the 20-35 model. Production of the 20-35 continued until 1929, and at that time it was replaced with the Model E, 25-40 tractor. This early advertisement indicated that the 20-35 sold for $1,295 cash, f.o.b. the factory. Instead of full cash payment, the buyer could arrange other payment terms, but this increased the total price. Deep green with red striping characterized these early models; the famous Persian Orange wouldn't come until 1929.

Here's Jim Polacek of Phillips, Wisconsin, heading home after a hard day's threshing with his Allis-Chalmers Model U tractor. Following is his 1948 Belle City threshing machine. This particular Model U was built in 1934, and is shown here on factory rubber. The Model U became famous as the first production farm tractor offered with low pressure rubber tires. This popular A-C model was built from 1929 to 1952, with well over 20,000 copies produced. Evident also is a small idler pulley mounted over the front axle. This kept the drive belt from rubbing on the axle. The tractors from U-1 to U-7404 (1929-1932) were built with a Continental engine. Later models carried an engine built by Allis-Chalmers. To publicize the new rubber tires, Allis-Chalmers sent the tractors to county fairs. These tractors were equipped with special gearing for "high speed" races. In fact, the famous Barney Oldfield covered a measured mile at a speed of 64.28mph in 1933. That must have been some ride!

Another fine example of a restored Model U tractor is illustrated by owner Edwin Karg of Hutchinson, Minnesota. This one is entirely on steel, and in fact, purchasers had the option of buying either steel wheels or rubber tires at least until 1940. In fact, due to the scarcity of rubber during World War II, many tractors were available from the factory only with steel wheels. After the hostilities had ended, owners could buy rubber tires once again. Many of the Model U tractors originally equipped with steel wheels were later "cut down" and equipped with rubber tires. Local welding shops simply cut off the steel wheel and welded the remaining spokes to new rims.

This Model U tractor was sold new in 1930 through the Cockshutt Plow Company in Canada. The price was $1,050 Canadian. It is owned by Ivan Henderson of Ontario, Canada. Model U tractors were first built with a Continental engine, but this was later changed to an Allis-Chalmers engine. Rated at 1,200rpm, it carried a 4½x5in bore and stroke. This tractor developed slightly over 35 brake horsepower in Nebraska test number 170. It also made a maximum pull of 3,679lb. Considering that it weighed 4,821lb, it pulled an amazing 76 percent of its own weight.

In Nebraska test number 237 of 1935, dual drawbar tests were run on the Model U tractor. Earlier models carried a Continental engine, but when A-C began using their own engine, a new test was required. In this case, 33.18 brake horsepower was elicited from the four-cylinder engine. Rated at 1,200rpm, it used a 4³/₈x5in bore and stroke. The test tractor was operated on distillate. Distillate can best be described as a poor gasoline, or a pretty fair kerosene. The distillate craze had run its course by 1950. The chief benefit of using distillate fuel was crankcase dilution, meaning that distillate getting past the rings ended up in the crankcase oil to the detriment of proper lubrication.

This fine restoration is the work of owner Alan Draper, Bishopstone of Salisbury, Wiltshire, Great Britain. Built in 1936, the Model U is shown in a harvest field. The Allis-Chalmers Model UM engine used in this series gained wide respect. It was thoroughly reliable, caused few problems, and could run for years without an overhaul, given of course, a good maintenance program. Allis-Chalmers offered this same engine as a stationary power unit for many years, and thousands were sold. While the majority of Allis-Chalmers Model U tractors were sold on the domestic market, considerable numbers were exported. The company had previously established worldwide contacts through its other industries, and it appears that their international market for steam turbines, electric generators, and other equipment was conducive to establishing the overseas tractor market.

One of the most famous of all A-C publicity shots was that of the first Allis-Chalmers Model U tractor to be equipped with rubber tires. A-C began experimenting with pneumatic tires by 1930, and in April 1932 the company mounted a pair of Firestone 48x12 airplane tires on a Model U tractor owned by Albert Schroeder of Waukesha, Wisconsin. This was so successful that A-C held demonstrations all over the country, and rubber tires became standard equipment for the Model U tractors in 1932.

Larry Karg of Hutchinson, Minnesota, puts his 1935 Model UC in gear. The high belly clearance and the clean lines made this an excellent row-crop tractor. When equipped with rubber tires, the UC had a top road speed of 10mph. However, when equipped with steel wheels, a simple gear lockout in the transmission prevented the use of this gear. The tractor was restored by Larry and Edwin Karg.

A close-up of the Allis-Chalmers Model UC tractor illustrates the impressive powerplant. Also evident is the cast-iron oil pan, and the simple, straightforward, unit design. The four-cylinder engine was equipped with a Bendix-Scintilla magneto and a Zenith K-5 carburetor as standard equipment. Bendix-Scintilla was noted for their experience in aircraft ignition. When this technology was applied to tractor magnetos, an excellent magneto resulted.

The Allis-Chalmers All-Crop

The Allis-Chalmers All-Crop has everything the farmer needs in a general purpose tractor . . . It has power to pull three 14″ plows at 3⅓ miles per hour in average soil conditions . . . It has the famous five-minute cultivator change feature . . . It has easy-working, convenient controls, and a steering mechanism that is as sensitive to the touch as a truck or automobile . . . It has perfect balance — economy of performance — and built-in long life.

The All-Crop is more of a working companion than a cold-blooded machine.

Previous page
The A-C Model UC of 1930-1941 was also billed as the Allis-Chalmers All-Crop tractor. This 1932 illustration uses this designation, although it appears that subsequent advertising simply used the UC designator. The design's simplicity is evident, with sturdiness of design also apparent. Due to the company's broad experience in the heavy equipment industries, Allis-Chalmers had been early to develop high-strength castings and forgings. In this respect, Allis-Chalmers was somewhat ahead of its peers, at least for a few years.

Production of the Allis-Chalmers Model A tractor ran from 1936 to 1942. This standard-tread model sold poorly compared to the popular WC tractor or to most other tractors of the A-C line. Rated at 1000rpm, it used a $4^3/_4$x$6^1/_2$in, four-cylinder engine. Total weight was 7,120lb. For reasons unknown, this tractor model was never tested at the Tractor Test Laboratory in Lincoln, Nebraska.

Production of the famous Model WC tractors began in 1933. From 1933-1948, Allis-Chalmers built over 178,000 of these truly useful tractors. Rated at 24hp, it could pull a two-bottom plow under almost all conditions, and could even pull a three-bottom plow with favorable circumstances. This copy is of 1942 vintage and is owned by Ivan Henderson of Cambridge, Ontario, Canada.

Allis-Chalmers began production of the little Model B tractor in 1937. It remained in production for twenty years. In Great Britain, production ended in 1955. Until mid-1940, an electric starter and lights were not standard equipment, but came as extra-cost options. After this time, however, these options were part of the standard package. In 1940 the Model B, complete with electrical system and 9-24 rear tires, retailed at $570. The adjustable-width front axle was a $20 option. The rear-mounted belt pulley and pto shaft added another $35 to the total price. This tractor is owned by Ivan Henderson.

Next page
This Allis-Chalmers Model B tractor was built in 1947 at the Totton Works near Southampton in Great Britain. In 1948, the local Allis-Chalmers plant converted the tractor for use in the orchards of Kent. They converted it by turning the final drive castings through 90 degrees and altering the front kingpins. This shortened the wheelbase and lowered the tractor by about 10in. They modified all the brake rods, pedals, steering, seat, and rear wings. This Orchard B was popular in the fruit tree farms of Great Britain. It is owned and was restored by Alan Cannings of Lewes, England.

Allis-Chalmers built a substantial number of tractors at Totton Works in Great Britain. Included was this Model B now owned by G. Stephens. Allis-Chalmers dealers became active in Great Britain during the early 1930s, and they sold the A-C farm equipment line extensively in that country for many years. Some A-C tractor models sold in Great Britain carried different model designators than ones on tractors sold in the United States.

Allis-Chalmers built the Model B tractor from 1937 to 1957. During this twenty-year period, the company manufactured over 127,000 copies. A-C also built the Model IB tractor, which was an industrial version. When production of the IB ended in 1955, only about 3,400 had been sent into the field. This is the Alan Cannings tractor that was converted into an Orchard model in 1948.

Previous page
Between 1940 and 1950 Allis-Chalmers built
some 84,000 Model C tractors. This popular
model featured slightly more horsepower
than the Model B. Even though Allis-
Chalmers pioneered rubber tires for tractors,
and even though rubber tires offered many
advantages over steel wheels, the Model C
was also available on steel wheels for those
of this persuasion. During World War II,
A-C built a limited number with steel
wheels, simply because no rubber tires were
available!

This 1948 Allis-Chalmers Model C tractor is
equipped with a bench seat. Although the
back support is present, there are no side
supports. The company staked much of its
short-term future on the Model C tractor.
Many different implements were built
especially for use with the Model C,
including a wide range of planters, plows,
and cultivators. The Model C was first tested
at Nebraska in 1940, using distillate fuel,
under test number 363. The following test,
number 364 was run on the same tractor,
but this time using gasoline fuel. Burning
gasoline, it developed nearly 19 maximum
brake horsepower.

In the States it's called a cultivator, but in Canada and other countries, it's called a scuffler. Semantics aside, here's a 1949 Model C Allis-Chalmers equipped with a 1941 A-C cultivator still used by Ivan Henderson. Allis-Chalmers built an extensive series of implements for the Model C tractor. This tractor model was ideally suited for the small farm, as well as for the commercial gardener, the small truck garden, and other duties.

Ivan Henderson sits at the controls of his A-C WD tractor. The power-adjustable rear wheels, the totally independent pto clutch, and other forward features made the WD immensely popular. In seven years of production, A-C built over 160,000 units. This tractor used a four-cylinder, 201ci engine with a 4in bore and stroke. It was tested at Nebraska in 1948 under number 399, and tested again in 1950 under number 440. The latter test yielded over 32 belt horsepower.

Because over 160,000 WD tractors were built, a considerable number still exist today. This is due not only to the large number built, but also to their durability. As previously noted, the WD was a direct-line descendant of the earlier WC tractor. The WC model was a major force in bringing about the change from heavy tractors with excess iron to powerful tractors using a minimum of weight. As an early tractor engineer once noted, "For too many years we sold too much iron for too little money."

This restored WD was photographed at the Old Time Threshing & Antique Engine Show, Freeport, Illinois. Sitting on his 1949 Allis-Chalmers WD is Marvin Holmes of Savanna, Illinois. Mounted on the rear is a nice looking leveling blade built by Holmes. Three front-end options were available for the WD tractors: the tricycle front, the adjustable wide-front axle, and the single-wheel front, sometimes called a "donut-wheel" front.

The Model RC tractor was probably intended to be a competitor to Harvester's concurrent F-14 tractor. It had a WC chassis and drivetrain powered by a 125ci engine as used in the Model B and Model C tractors. Introduced in 1939, the ill-fated RC tractor was out of production in 1941, and did not resume after World War II. Since the RC tractor essentially used a WC chassis, the specialized implements built for the WC fit on this tractor. The Allis-Chalmers RC tractor was tested at Nebraska in 1939 under number 316. The slightly lower price of the RC, compared to the larger WC model, was apparently an inadequate motivation for tractor buyers. Likewise, those farmers needing the smaller Model C tractor saw little advantage in paying even slightly more for the only slightly larger RC. Thus, the company's hopes for the RC soon evaporated.

Production of the Model WF tractor began in 1937 and continued until 1951. This tractor was a standard-tread, fixed-width version of the WC row-crop model. However, the WC was also available with an adjustable wide-front axle as an option over the standard tricycle design. Like the WC, this model used an Allis-Chalmers W engine having a 4-inch bore and stroke. The WF tractors were available with steel wheels, rubber tires, or rear steel and rubber fronts.

A rear view of the Model WF tractor illustrates its clean lines. Essentially, Allis-Chalmers used the engine and front half of the WC chassis with a slightly different rear-end design. The sheet metal differs only a little, and the seat design is virtually the same. No WF tractors were built in 1943, but production resumed the following year and continued until 1951. For 1948 the WF tractor listed at $971 on steel. The same model equipped with rubber tires sold for $1,210. This model was never tested at Nebraska. When operating on kerosene or distillate fuels, it was essential to maintain the engine temperature at a reasonably high level. Operating at low jacket temperatures was a major factor in contributing to crankcase oil dilution by the fuel due to condensation. Kerosene does not vaporize in the same manner as gasoline; in fact, at standard operating temperatures, atomization is closer to the reality. This radiator shutter decal informs the operator to maintain the water temperature at a minimum of 170 degrees Fahrenheit for gasoline and 190 degrees when operating on distillate or tractor fuel.

Ivan Henderson of Ontario, Canada, displays his pride while astride his 1948 Model WF tractor. Only about 8,000 of these tractors were built between 1937 and 1951. The arched front axle permitted the operator to straddle growing row crops. Without the arch, crops of over 10 or 12in would be impossible to negotiate without serious damage, but with this feature, crops could be somewhat more mature and still be accessible for spraying and other work.

In 1953, Allis-Chalmers introduced their WD-45 tractor. It was the immediate successor to the Model WD, first built in 1948. The lineage went back even further to the Model WC tractor, introduced in 1933. This 1954 WD-45 includes hydraulic power and the power-adjustable rear wheels. In 1956, A-C enhanced the WD-45 by adding factory-installed power steering. The spin-out rear wheel design permitted easy changing of the tread width, using the tractor's own power. By comparison, most other tractors of the period still relied on loosening large hub bolts, and then driving the rusted hubs in or out with a block of wood and a sledgehammer. The A-C spin-out design eliminated these problems and permitted the changeover in a matter of minutes.

Although the tricycle front wheels were standard equipment, the WD and WD-45 tractors were also available with an adjustable wide-front axle. A wet clutch between the pto shaft and the transmission provided continuous pto power totally independent of ground travel. The main, foot-operated clutch disengaged both the transmission and the pto shaft. During 1953, Allis-Chalmers incorporated the Snap-Coupler system into the WD and CA tractors. With the system came an entire line of implements tailored to this new design.

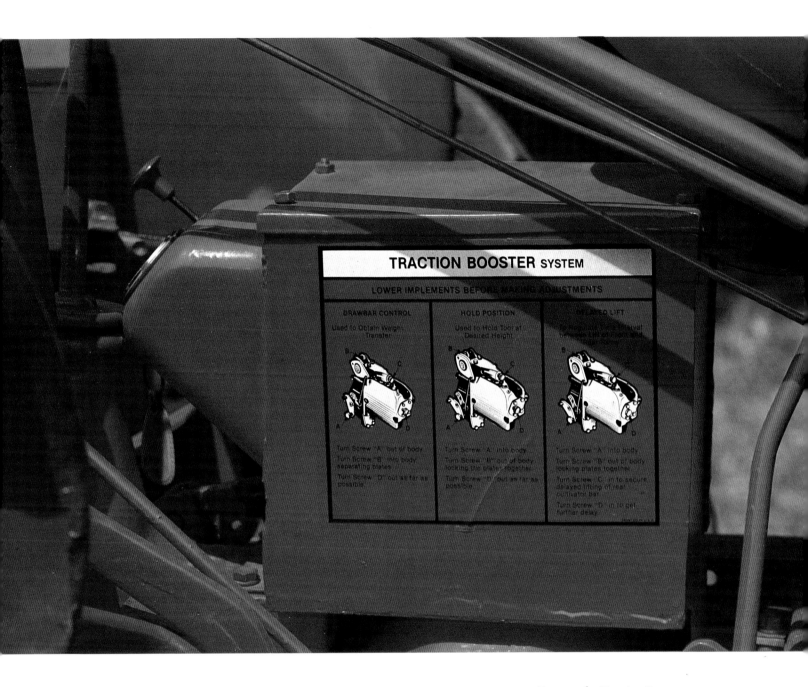

Because the Traction Booster system was a radically new design, Allis-Chalmers attached a special decal to the tractor. Shown here on the side of the battery box, this decal contained the essential information for efficient use of the Traction Booster. Including this detailed information was not unique for Allis-Chalmers. Many A-C tractors and implements carried informational decals; this idea was later adopted by other manufacturers.

In 1955, Allis-Chalmers introduced the WD-45 Diesel tractor. It used a six-cylinder 230ci engine rated at over 40 brake horsepower. Production of this model was rather limited, since it was only available in the 1955-1957 period. This copy is owned by Theodore Buisker of Davis, Illinois, who uses it on a daily basis in his farming operation. Buisker first drove a WD-45 Diesel when he was but five years old. The WD-45 Diesel, like other Allis-Chalmers tractors of the period, carried a distinctive designator decal. This six-cylinder tractor used a $3^7/_{16}$x$4^1/_8$in engine with a rated speed of 1625rpm. Its compression ratio was 15.5:1. Testing of the WD-45 Diesel is covered in Nebraska test number 563 of October 1955. This was the first instance of an Allis-Chalmers wheel tractor with a diesel engine. It carried a retail price of $3,400.

Allis-Chalmers had had considerable experience in engine building over the years, but this was greatly enhanced by the buy out of the Buda Company at Harvey, Illinois, in the early 1950s. From this factory, Allis-Chalmers continued building engines by the thousands, not only for its own tractors and equipment, but also under contract to OEM manufacturers and for military purposes. Buda had been a pioneer in the development of high-speed diesels. Some of these innovations were built into the durable WD-45 Diesel engine shown here.

Next page
Here's a 1956 Model WD-45 restored by Earl Smith of Manville, Illinois. (The customer wanted the non-original radial RVT front tires.) Allis-Chalmers tractors are always popular at vintage tractor pulls, and seem to have an uncanny pulling ability for their size and weight.

During the 1950s, most farm tractor manufacturers offered propane versions as an alternative to gasoline engines. Each had advantages and disadvantages, but the transition to diesel engines eventually ended the domination of all spark-fired engines.

Production of the Allis-Chalmers CA tractor began in 1950. This model replaced the Model C, which had gone into production ten years earlier. This 1954 model was in the 26hp class. Standard equipment on this copy includes the Traction Booster hitch system, the Snap Coupler quick-hitch, and a hand-controlled clutch. It is owned by Ivan Henderson.

Production of the Allis-Chalmers Model G began in 1948. Designed especially for small farms, vegetable gardeners, and landscapers, the Model G was a small compact tractor that A-C called the "central unit of a new system of motorized farm tools." This new system was as good as its word. Allis-Chalmers built an entire array of implements tailored especially for the Model G's unique design. The Model G tractor was produced at the Gadsden, Alabama, works. The Model G tractor featured a rear-mounted engine of

four-cylinder design. The engine was a Continental N-62 with a 2⅜x3½in bore and stroke. Allis-Chalmers sent a copy of the Model G to the Nebraska Tractor Test Laboratory in 1948, and it was tested under number 398. In this test, the Model G delivered 9.6 drawbar and 10.9 belt horsepower. The belt pulley was a $19 option, and a hydraulic system was available for an additional $99. In 1955, the last year of production, the Model G listed at $970. This is a nicely restored Model G equipped

with a cultivator designed especially for the tractor. Allis-Chalmers attempted to promote the Model G for the soybean farmer. The company issued a special catalog that illustrated a two-row drill planter for soybeans. One-, two-, and three-row tool bar cultivators were also available in a variety of configurations to suit virtually any cultivating need. This attractive restoration is owned by Ivan Henderson of Cambridge, Ontario, Canada.

Allis-Chalmers had major plans for the small Model G tractor. Built between 1948 and 1955, production fell short of expectations with less than 30,000 completed. For truck farmers and certain other operations the Model G was immensely popular, but for the average grain farmer, the Model G never gained great popularity. This 1950s photograph shows a Model G with a front-mounted swather or windrower.

The popular D-17 tractor saw first light in 1957. With the introduction of the D Series tractors, Allis-Chalmers ended the long career of the WC, WD, and WD-45 models. This new model built on the successes of the past, and incorporated many new designs as well. The first revision, called Series II began in 1959, the Series III tractors were introduced in 1964, followed by the Series IV models in 1965.

Allis-Chalmers introduced its immensely popular D-17 tractor in 1957. In addition to the initial design, three subsequent versions appeared: the Series II, beginning in 1959; the Series III beginning in 1964; and the Series IV beginning in 1965. Production ended in 1967. Shown here is a 1966 D-17 Series IV tractor cutting hay on a 100 degree day.

Previous page
Allis-Chalmers D-17 tractors had three different engine styles. In addition to the standard four-cylinder gasoline model, A-C could modify the D-17 for propane gas (at an additional cost). For either fuel, the engine was essentially the same, except that special equipment was required for propane. The company could also make the D-17 with a six-cylinder diesel engine. Shown is a 1958 D-17. The D Series tractors featured the Power Director Clutch, Traction Booster, and the A-C Power-Crater engine. A four-cylinder engine was used in the gasoline and propane versions. Both carried a 4x4½in bore and stroke for a displacement of 226ci. (The same G-226 engine was sold extensively as a stationary or portable power unit.) The gasoline model used a compression ratio of 7.5:1, but this was raised to 8.5:1 for the propane version.

This overhead view shows the complete A-C line of about 1960. The array was assembled for a sales training school at the Allis-Chalmers farm near Racine, Wisconsin. A-C dealers, territory men, and factory people attended. In this way, the dealer could bring the latest developments to the customer. Although Allis-Chalmers had earlier been identified as a manufacturer of tractors and the All-Crop combine, the company developed an exceptionally complete implement line during the 1950s.

Larry and Edwin Karg of Hutchinson, Minnesota, own this 1962 D-15 tractor. Built between 1960 and 1967, this model saw production of well over 20,000 copies. Allis-Chalmers built D-15 tractors, prior to serial number 9001 of 1962, with a four-cylinder, $3\frac{1}{2}$x$3\frac{7}{8}$in engine. After this number, A-C increased the bore to $3\frac{5}{8}$in. Although some company documents indicate that the D-15 Series II tractors did not appear until 1965, other references point to the increased horsepower output resulting from the 1962

engine modifications as the likely beginning of the Series II tractors. Although this photograph was taken in 1991, the scene is reminiscent of a typical A-C dealership of the 1960s. In the background is the familiar A-C diamond trademark the company used from its 1901 beginnings. The diamond underwent subsequent changes and modifications, but it nevertheless remained on all Allis-Chalmers products from the smallest tractor to the largest steam turbine.

In 1963 Allis-Chalmers offered the ED-40 tractor to the Canadian market. This model carried a 138ci diesel engine. Heater plug starting equipment was standard, as was the Category I, three-point lift. Production was apparently limited to 1963. No serial number or production data has been located for this tractor. However, the serial number location is under the seat on the transmission's left side.

Edwin Karg of Hutchinson, Minnesota, is semi-retired and spends his spare time restoring Allis-Chalmers D Series tractors with his son, Larry. Shown here is their 1959 D-12 tractor. Like many D Series tractors, the D-12 underwent various changes. Effective with serial number 3501, A-C increased the D-12 engine's bore to 3^1/$_2$in. A-C equipped the original model with a four-cylinder engine and a bore and stroke of 3^3/$_8$x3^7/$_8$in. An A-C instruction manual stated, "The Model D-10 and D-12 tractors are similar in most respects with the exception of the tread. The Model D-10 has the narrower tread and is designed for one-row cultivation. The D-12 has the wider wheel tread and is designed for two-row cultivation. Both models are available in high clearance design." Production of the D-10 ran from 1959 to 1967. This 1961 version is still used for plowing.

Previous page
Built from 1959 to 1967, the D-10 was quite similar to the D-12. As with most other tractors in the D-Series, the D-10 was available in a high-clearance model in addition to the standard configuration shown here. The D-10 models built after serial number 3501 of 1961 carried a 3¹/₂in cylinder bore, compared to the 3³/₈x3⁷/₈in bore and stroke on the original version. Thus, the original 139ci displacement was raised to 149ci. The latter engine, when sold for stationary duty, was known as the Model G-149. Thousands were built and sold.

Allis-Chalmers did much work at its experimental farm outside of West Allis. The company also sent out experimental and preproduction tractors to selected operators for their evaluation. By these and other means, A-C could work out any problems prior to full production. This D-12 Series III tractor, built from 1964 to 1967 and equipped with a two-row, rear-mounted cultivator, cultivates soybeans at the Allis-Chalmers farm near Racine, Wisconsin.

Production of the D-19 tractor ran only from 1961 to 1963. During that time, A-C assigned only 11,000 serial numbers. This model could be purchased for use with gasoline, LP-gas, or diesel fuels. The diesel engine was, of course, entirely different, while the LP-gas version was simply a modification of the basic gasoline engine. Production of the D-19 LP-gas model was rather limited, particularly since this type of fuel required special equipment for refueling, which was an added expense to the operator. Finding a suitable location for the gas storage tank was a problem, and although this one has been specially built to fit the space provided, it nevertheless tends to obstruct vision to some degree.

Next page
The Allis-Chalmers D-19 tractor was built in the 1961-1963 period. Production totaled about 11,000 units. This model delivered over 71 maximum pto horsepower in Nebraska Tractor test number 810, and featured the A-C-built Model G262 engine. In addition to the gasoline version, A-C also built the D-19 with a 262ci turbocharged four-cylinder diesel engine. The D-19 gasoline model listed at about $5,300, while the D-19 diesel tractor sold for about $6,000. Both were available as high-clearance models, and this option added about $1,000 to the list price. Allis-Chalmers diesel tractors were often turbocharged, A-C pioneered the use of turbochargers on farm tractors. Adding this feature increased the horsepower about 20 percent over naturally aspirated engines.

Allis-Chalmers built the D-21 Series II tractors from 1965 to 1969. A major difference was the change from the Model 3400 naturally aspirated engine to the Model 3500 turbocharged style. Rated at 2200rpm, this style boasted a 426ci displacement. Like other D Series tractors of the period, the D-21 used a dry air cleaner. Allis-Chalmers was one of the first tractor builders to feature dry air cleaners instead of the customary oil bath style.

Production of the big D-21 tractor began in 1963. Built only as a diesel model, it featured the newly designed A-C Model 3400 engine. The early production was naturally aspirated, but a turbocharger soon became standard equipment. The naturally aspirated model was tested at Nebraska under number 855 of October 1963. At one point in production, Allis-Chalmers experimented with a front-wheel-assist design, apparently using hydraulic motors within the front wheels.

Here's a D-21 tractor with an A-C number 2541 rear-mounted cultivator. This eight-row style cultivates soybeans at the Allis-Chalmers farm near Racine, Wisconsin. This large tractor had a bare weight of about 9,700lb, and the turbocharged model developed over 127 pto horsepower, with a delivery of about 116hp at the drawbar. In addition to the agricultural model shown here, the D-21 was also built in an industrial version.

With the close out of the successful D Series tractors in the late 1960s, Allis-Chalmers introduced an entirely new tractor line with number designators. Included were the 170, 175, 180, 185, 190, and 190XT models. The Model 180 shown here was built from 1968 to 1973. In the four-plow category, users could purchase the Model 180 in gasoline or diesel versions or as an industrial model. The gasoline style used the A-C Model G-2500 engine; six cylinders with a 3¾x4in bore and stroke. The diesel model carried an A-C Model 2800 engine with a maximum output of 64.01 pto horsepower.

During the late 1970s, Allis-Chalmers built the 70 Series tractors, including the 7040 and 7060 tractors shown here. A Model 6070 tractor was the last one Allis-Chalmers built; it left the production line on December 6, 1985.

Chapter 5

Allis-Chalmers Implements and Combines

The Farmer's Helping Hand From Plows to the All-Crop Harvesters

The development of the Allis-Chalmers farm implement line initially came about through the acquisition of previously established companies. From these roots, A-C went on to provide the farmer with some of the most innovative designs of the period.

A major example is the development of the All-Crop combine. Until 1930, the majority of small grain was cut, shocked, and threshed as it had been for decades. A few combines were in use, but these machines were so large that they were suitable only for large acreages. Allis-Chalmers set out to change that idea, and succeeded with the All-Crop combine. This small machine was a fraction of the weight of earlier designs, and was priced within the reach of the average farmer. A

During the 1930s and 1940s, Allis-Chalmers emerged as an innovator in the farm implement business. Within a few short years, A-C developed an extensive implement line, tailor-made for specific crops and centered around specific tractor models.

A head-on view illustrates the 1940 Allis-Chalmers corn pickers. These direct-attached pickers were still experimental at that point, but were designed to "sell for about half the price of those on the market, yet they will work better." To the left is a WC tractor with a two-row mounted style, and on the right is a Model B tractor with a one-row mounted picker. Note that it is mounted in the center of the tractor, with the snapping rolls just beneath the radiator.

This WD tractor pulls an A-C forage harvester, cutting green alfalfa in full bloom. Allis-Chalmers produced this machine for several years. Despite its unique appearance, when compared to competing machines the A-C forage harvester was a successful venture. A built-in knife grinder was standard equipment. This made it easy to maintain the cutter knives with a razor-sharp edge. Allowing them to run dull greatly increased the horsepower required, and chances are that this WD had all the load it needed and then some!

small engine or a tractor's own power takeoff shaft could run the combine.

In addition to its compact design, the All-Crop offered many features unavailable in other combines, small or large. The special cylinder design permitted the successful harvesting of virtually any seed crop. This feature alone made the All-Crop worth its weight in gold to the farmer. Now it was possible to harvest clover, alfalfa, or timothy seed, and then change over to wheat, oats, or soybeans. The All-Crop design contin-

ued through numerous models in the following years.

In 1955, A-C purchased the Gleaner Harvester Company, and from that point on, Allis-Chalmers gained instant recognition with its Gleaner combines.

Development of the A-C Roto-Baler was another design unique to the farm equipment industry. The idea for the round bale originated many years before, but the Roto-Baler of 1947 was the rage of the farming community. The small round bales were good at shedding moisture,

and the baler was reasonably priced. Eventually the company built conventional hay balers, and phased out the Roto-Baler design.

During its years in the farm implement business, Allis-Chalmers pioneered other farm machinery innovations, including the drive-in cultivator, and the drive-in corn picker mounting.

The revolutionary new cylinder system used in the Model 60 combine permitted the harvesting of clover, alfalfa, and other seed crops with relative ease. By comparison, the ordinary threshing machine was unable to do so in an efficient manner. Thus, the

clover huller was generally used for these crops. Here, a Model B tractor pulls a Model 60 combine in a clover seed harvest. Due to the lack of tractor power in the Model B, this combine is equipped with its own power unit.

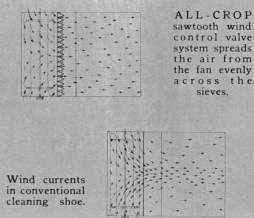

The ALL-CROP cleaning shoe, showing wind control, two adjustable chaffers and one finishing sieve.

ALL-CROP sawtooth wind control valve system spreads the air from the fan evenly across the sieves.

Wind currents in conventional cleaning shoe.

Expert Cleaning
MADE EASY

IT DOESN'T take a veteran thresherman to get expertly-cleaned grain, beans, or seed from the ALL-CROP harvester. Even a beginner can master the simple wind-control, chaffer and sieve adjustments, and learn to set them correctly for thorough cleaning without waste.

Only the ALL-CROP has the highly efficient sawtooth wind-control valve system, which regulates the volume of air entering the cleaning shoe and distributes the blast uniformly across the full width of the sieves.

This system of wind-control, because of the saw-tooth design, does away with unwelcome cross-blasts and other unwanted air disturbances common to machines using the old system of hand-adjusted wind-control blinds in the sides of the fan housing. Regardless of the direction or intensity of the wind outside, or the position of the machine in relation to it as it cuts around the field, the air-blast in the

cleaning shoe remains constant in volume and distribution. It is also possible to direct the air-blast to the front or rear of the sieves to meet the requirements of any crop or condition. These features assure consistently good cleaning under all conditions.

Standard equipment includes one adjustable chaffer, one adjustable sieve, and one finishing sieve. Additional finishing sieves to meet the requirements of beans, small grains, or seed of any size, shape or variety are obtainable at small extra cost. You can do top-notch cleaning in any crop with the ALL-CROP.

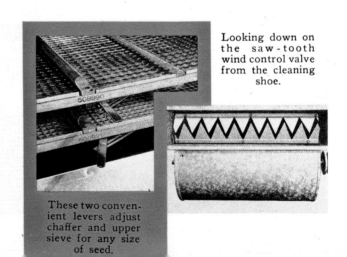

Looking down on the saw-tooth wind control valve from the cleaning shoe.

These two convenient levers adjust chaffer and upper sieve for any size of seed.

Red Clover

Hop Clover

Onion Seed

Lespedeza

Brome Grass

Flax

Safflower

Kaffir

Wheat

Rice

Barley

Oats

Rye

Buckwheat

Soy Beans

Pinto Beans

Truly an

ALL-CROP

Harvester

THE ALL-CROP harvester lives up to its name, for it has successfully harvested more than 100 different small-grain, bean, seed, and sorghum crops under actual farm conditions. No single farmer, of course, has that many crops to harvest, but it is not uncommon to find farmers who grow as many as three to eight different crops and harvest all of them with an ALL-CROP.

Here's the list of crops that the Model "60" has successfully harvested. Check the grains, beans, sorghums, grass and legume seed crops you grow now . . . and those you may want to grow some day.

Small Grains

Barley
Oats
Rice
  Common
  Red
Rye
Spelt
Wheat

Legumes

Alfalfa
Beans
  Baby Lima
  Black Eye
  Bountiful
  Clay Bank
  Cranberry
  Ebony
  Faba or Horse
  Garvanzo
  Great Northern
  Italian
  Kentucky Wonder
  Kidney
  Mung
  Navy
  Pinto
  Red Mexican

Soy
Velvet
Clovers
  Alsike
  Birdsfoot Trefoil
  Crimson
  Dutch
  Giant English
  Hop
  Hubam
  Ladino
  Persian
  Red
  Sweet
  White
Crotalaria
Lespedeza
  Kobe
  Korean
  Sericea
  Tennessee "76"
Peas
  Alaska
  Austrian
  Chinese Red
  Cow
  Lady
  Table
  Whipoorwill
Vetch

Grasses

Bent
Bermuda
Big Blue Stem
Blue
Brome
Canadian Rye
Canary
Carpet
Crested Wheat
Dallis
English Rye
Grama
Indian Rice
Johnson
Millet
  Common
  Hog or Proso
Orchard
Red Top
Rhodes
Sudan
Sand Drop
Timothy
Western Wheat

Sorghums

Cane
Hegari
Kaffir
Sorgo

Broom
Gyp
Maize

Seeds

Beets
  Table
  Sugar
Cabbage
Carrot
Buckwheat
Chicory
Fenugreek
Flax
Fuzzy Cheat
Lettuce
Mustard
Onions
Okra
Parsnip
Poppy
Radish
Rape
Safflower
Sagrain
Spinach
Sunflower
Tobacco
Turnip
Zinnia

Previous page
In 1935 the Allis-Chalmers All-Crop combine made its appearance. A-C registered the All-Crop trademark on its combine in 1935, and for some years the bright orange All-Crop helped bring an end to grain binders and threshing machines. With its five-foot cut, the Model 60 could be powered with the WC tractor, or others within its horsepower class. As an option, the Model 60 could be equipped with its own engine.

A 1950s photograph illustrates products built at the La Porte Works. The old Rumely factories are situated next to a lake. Legend has it that when workers erected one of the factory buildings, an OilPull tractor was buried due to a cave-in of the soft ground. Rumor has it that the tractor has remained entombed ever since. In the foreground and to the right is the unique front-unloading manure spreader Allis-Chalmers designed and built.

Production of the small Model 40 combine ran from 1938 to 1940. This 1938 photograph illustrates the Model 40 production line at the La Porte, Indiana, works. Starting on one side, the harvester soon takes definite shape as it passes down the automatic conveyor line. The La Porte works was able to build 150 of these machines per day.

Only about 4,500 units of the Allis-Chalmers Model 72 All-Crop combine were built between 1959 and 1962. The D-14 auxiliary engine was used when a power unit was required. In 1960, the Model 72 was priced at $1,898. This Model 72 is in tow behind a D-15 diesel tractor.

In 1955, Allis-Chalmers purchased the Gleaner Harvester Company, which had been in the combine business for years. The buy out put Allis-Chalmers squarely into the market. Even though the All-Crop met with tremendous success initially, the market for small combines disappeared by the early 1950s. Farmers simply wanted larger combines, and the new self-propelled models became more and more important to the industry. Shown here are a pair of Model C Gleaner combines working in Texas.

Allis-Chalmers introduced their famous Roto-Baler in 1947. It followed designs that had been around for decades, but with the Roto-Baler the concept of "round bales" gained momentum. This machine remained in production until 1960, although production diminished to a fraction of that enjoyed in the early years. Curiously, Allis-Chalmers left the round baler business just before the concept of large round bales appeared.

Chapter 6

Collecting Allis-Chalmers

The Ongoing Legacy of Persian Orange

Anyone collecting old tractors in the 1950s was thought of as a bit odd, to say the least. Ten years later, tractor collectors got silent assent, but with a good bit of tongue clucking and nodding of heads. By the 1970s, tractor collecting finally gained recognition and respectability. In the 1990s, tractor collecting and restoration has become a popular hobby.

It is interesting that many of today's tractor collectors go to great lengths to

This Allis-Chalmers Model U tractor was built in 1937 and features the A-C Model UM engine. Of overhead valve design, the Model U was exceptionally popular, due perhaps in part, to its coat of bright orange paint. Some speculate that Harry Merritt, chief engineer of the Tractor Division, chose this color to match the bright orange California poppies. This tractor is in the Ivan Henderson collection.

pedigree their prizes. They like to know where their tractor comes from, in other words, its working history. They want to know how many were built. Many collectors can even determine when minor changes and modifications were made in the design.

Depending on the make and model, many antique and classic tractors sought by today's collectors are difficult to restore. Since most enthusiasts opt for a total restoration, the search for engine parts can sometimes take months or years to accomplish successfully. Restoration of the mechanical components is only one aspect of the job. Rebuilding a vintage tractor includes repairing and replacing tinwork and recovering the steering wheel.

After hours of work, the tractor finally is ready for paint. Although some collectors paint their own tractors, today's acrylics and high-tech finishes often demand that the collector send the

tractor to a professional. (Some shops even specialize in restoring old tractors.)

Once the paint job is complete, the collector applies a new set of decals. Many times, the tractor company is out of business or no longer makes new decals. So the collector searches for aftermarket decal sets. In some cases, it is necessary to hire a professional sign painter to paint the lettering.

Restoring a vintage tractor requires time and patience. Yet, it has become a rewarding pastime for collectors all over the world. While thousands of collectors reside in the United States, thousands more live in Canada. Tractor restoration has become a popular hobby in England, Australia, New Zealand, and in many European countries as well. A great many are general collectors who sport a bevy of different makes. Then there are those who specialize in a certain make, such as the Allis-Chalmers collectors featured within this book.

Ivan Henderson, an A-C collector in Cambridge, Ontario, lined up part of his fine collection just in time for the evening sun. From left to right are a 1948 Model WF tractor; a 1954 Model WD-45; a 1942 Model WC; and a rare 1939 Model RC. In the past few years, the ever-popular Allis-Chalmers tractor models have attracted increasing numbers of vintage tractor collectors. Some collectors specialize strictly in the bright Persian Orange tractors A-C built.

Index